The Green Dura...

Marisa Gonzales

The Green Burial Movement

LAP LAMBERT Academic Publishing

Impressum / Imprint
Bibliografische Information der Deutschen Nationalbibliothek: Die Deutsche Nationalbibliothek verzeichnet diese Publikation in der Deutschen Nationalbibliografie; detaillierte bibliografische Daten sind im Internet über http://dnb.d-nb.de abrufbar.
Alle in diesem Buch genannten Marken und Produktnamen unterliegen warenzeichen-, marken- oder patentrechtlichem Schutz bzw. sind Warenzeichen oder eingetragene Warenzeichen der jeweiligen Inhaber. Die Wiedergabe von Marken, Produktnamen, Gebrauchsnamen, Handelsnamen, Warenbezeichnungen u.s.w. in diesem Werk berechtigt auch ohne besondere Kennzeichnung nicht zu der Annahme, dass solche Namen im Sinne der Warenzeichen- und Markenschutzgesetzgebung als frei zu betrachten wären und daher von jedermann benutzt werden dürften.

Bibliographic information published by the Deutsche Nationalbibliothek: The Deutsche Nationalbibliothek lists this publication in the Deutsche Nationalbibliografie; detailed bibliographic data are available in the Internet at http://dnb.d-nb.de.
Any brand names and product names mentioned in this book are subject to trademark, brand or patent protection and are trademarks or registered trademarks of their respective holders. The use of brand names, product names, common names, trade names, product descriptions etc. even without a particular marking in this works is in no way to be construed to mean that such names may be regarded as unrestricted in respect of trademark and brand protection legislation and could thus be used by anyone.

Coverbild / Cover image: www.ingimage.com

Verlag / Publisher:
LAP LAMBERT Academic Publishing
ist ein Imprint der / is a trademark of
OmniScriptum GmbH & Co. KG
Heinrich-Böcking-Str. 6-8, 66121 Saarbrücken, Deutschland / Germany
Email: info@lap-publishing.com

Herstellung: siehe letzte Seite /
Printed at: see last page
ISBN: 978-3-8473-7388-9

Copyright © 2014 OmniScriptum GmbH & Co. KG
Alle Rechte vorbehalten. / All rights reserved. Saarbrücken 2014

The Green Burial Movement; Reworking the Relationship Between Death and Society

By Marisa Gonzales, M.A.

AKNOWLEDGMENTS

I would like to express my deepest thanks to Dr. Williams, my committee chair and mentor, for the encouragement, support and understanding. Without your guidance and structure this thesis would never have been possible.
Thank you to Dr. Sadri for your insight and appreciation of my cultural approach and for helping me to fine tune that perspective.
Huge thanks to Lona Choi-Allum for providing me the data.
To my mother, thank you for everything, especially for all of your support and instilment of the value of higher education. Thank you to my dad who has been my pillar of strength. To Reina, Roman, Sofia and Natalia you all keep me going and remember si se puede.
To Michan, friend and editor, thank you for sharing a passion for this topic and for your infinite literary resources.
Above all thank you to JC, for all that you have done for me. Words alone cannot express my full appreciation. And thanks for setting such a fine example.

ABSTRACT
MARISA GONZALES
GREEN BURIAL: REWORKING THE RELATIONSHIP BETWEEN DEATH AND SOCIETY
AUGUST 2009

This study explores the recently emerging green burial movement in the United States and the potential impact that it may have on American attitudes towards death and dying. This movement began as an alternative to costly and environmentally detrimental traditional burial practices. Expansion of this movement may contribute to a return to a more agrarian model of death could help to restructure the relationship between death and society.

To gain a better understanding of American attitudes towards green burial data from the 2007 AAPR Funeral and Burial Planners Survey were analyzed. Bivariate analysis was performed to identify the most significant predictors of support for green burial. Findings indicate that respondents with higher educational levels, higher SES standing, and younger respondents were more supportive of green burial. Implications of the findings are discussed and suggestions for future research are offered.

TABLE OF CONTENTS

ACKNOWLEDGEMENTS..i
ABSTRACT..ii
LIST OF TABLES.. iii
Chapters
  I.   INTRODUCTION..1
        Purpose of Study..1
        Rationale..4
  II.   REVIEW OF LITERATURE..6
        Funeral Industry..6
        History of Death Care Work......................................6
        Modern Death..8
        Historic Ethnography..12
            Dr. William Campbell......................................12
            Joe Shehee...14
            Don Brawley...16
            Jerrigrace Lyons..18
            Susanne Wiigh-Mäsak...................................19
        Green Burial..22
            Support for Environmental Movements....................22
                Income and Education.................................24
                Region and Urban/Rural Differences..................24
                Race..25
                Gender..26
  III. METHODOLOGY..27
        Data and Sample..27
        Variables...28
            Independent..28
            Dependent...28
        Research Questions...29
        Data Analysis..29
        Limitations..30
  IV. RESULTS...32
        Characteristics of Respondents.................................32

iv

	Research Questions..34
	Question 1...34
	Question 2...35
	Question 3...37
	Question 4...38
	Summary..39
V.	DISCUSSION..41
	Support of Green Burial...41
	Death as a Variable..43
	Environmentalism and the "Ethos of Waste"...........................44
	Death and Culture in America: Overcoming Social Distance............47
VI.	CONCLUSION..51
	Summary..51
	Implications...52
	Applications to the General Public..................................52
	Implications for the Funeral Industry..............................53
	Future of the Green Burial Movement............................54
	Future Research...55
	References...57

LIST OF TABLES

Table
1. Characteristics of Respondents..32
2. Support for Green Burial and Geographic Region......................34
3. Support for Green Burial and Income....................................35
4. Support for Green Burial and Education.................................37
5. Support for Green Burial and Age...38

CHAPTER I
INTRODUCTION

Purpose of the Study

Within the past fifty years, due in part to works such as Jessica Mitford's (1963) *The American Way of Death,* the American funeral industry has come under much scrutiny for its exploitation of the bereaved. Everything from the price of caskets to the necessity of embalming has been questioned and critiqued in both popular media and academia. Yet the idea of the traditional funeral is so closely associated with what is considered a "proper burial" (Davies 2005) and ingrained into American culture that few alternatives to the status quo have had much success. Within the past twenty years the discussion surrounding the American funeral industry has shifted from concern with the financially exploitative aspects of the business to that of its detrimental effects on the environment.

What is known today as traditional burial and preparation for burial practices in the United States began during a time period known as the "modernist era" of the early 1900's (Moller 1996). This era represented a transition from an overwhelmingly agrarian, pre-modern world to an industrial and modern one (Howarth and Jupp 1996).

Death in agrarian society was labeled by Moller as a "tame" death. By contrast, in the early industrial society of the time, death became something to be fought against, avoided in conversation and feared.

In terms of burial customs this transition was reflected in the removal of care of the deceased from the family and community to that of professionals, most commonly the undertaker. This removal of death from the public sector, or "social death" (Davies 2005), represented a drastic change in its meaning to and relationship with society. This was often utilized and manipulated by the funeral industry in their endeavor to "protect the public from the disorder of death and create the "magic" of a funeral" (Bartlett and Riches 2007).

In addition to the damage done to this relationship between society and death the effects of the funeral industry on the environment are immense. It is estimated that in each year 827,060 gallons of formaldehyde for embalming, 30 million feet of hardwood and 90,272 tons of steel for caskets, 14,000 tons of steel and 1,636,000 tons of reinforced concrete for vaults are buried in cemeteries across the United States (McClausland 2008).

Negative health effects due to exposure to harmful chemicals are also noted among workers within the funeral industry (Holness and Nethercott 1989).

In response to both the growing dissatisfaction with the traditional cultural approach to death as well as the environmental impact of the funeral industry, the "green burial" movement has developed (McCausland 2008). "Green burial" is a term that refers to burial and burial preparations choices that are more environmentally sound and require fewer natural resources than a traditional American funeral. Such options include burial without embalming the body, use of a burial shroud, cardboard or other biodegradable coffin or burial without a vault. These arrangements can be made and implemented by the family, a funeral director or with the assistance of a professional death midwife.

The green burial movement has gained substantial momentum over the past fifteen years. It is regarded as part of the larger environmental movement, one of the most successful social movements of the last half of the twentieth century both here in the U.S. as well as in Europe (Dalton 1994; Dunlap and Mertig 1992). This alternative offers its adherents both an environmentally friendly means of burial and an opportunity to reconstruct the relationship that American society has with death. Further, by this reconstruction of the relationship that individuals have with both the environment and death burial is no longer viewed as only a social and cultural ceremony, it additionally becomes considered for its function as a means of waste disposal (Wirzba 2003). Placing burial in this context may seem incomprehensible to a society that annually spends $20 billion each year on funerals (Stubbe 2007). However given growing concern over limited burial space and environmental contamination could cause the number of individuals interested in natural burial to increase.

The purpose of this thesis is to explore the green burial movement from a sociological perspective. More specifically, this thesis will use data from a recent survey provided by the AARP (American Association of Retired Persons) to examine predictors of support for green burial in the US. The goal is to gain a clearer perspective on characteristics of supporters of this movement.

Rationale

The green burial movement in the United States is a recent and still emerging social phenomenon modeled after similar movements in Great Britain and Canada (Kaufman 1998). Thus there is relatively little research of any sort available on this emerging movement. This thesis addresses the lack of literature that examines this subject and may be perhaps the first sociological study of the green burial movement. In addition, this study will shed light on changing American attitudes towards death and dying as a result of the growing alternative burial movement. Theoretically this movement is significant because it challenges traditional discourses on death. To date, sociologists interested in the issue of death and dying have given little, if any, sustained attention to such alternatives to traditional practices and beliefs regarding death and dying and to their implications for the way in which Americans think about and approach death. This thesis is an initial effort in this direction.

CHAPTER II
REVIEW OF LITERATURE

The first section reviews literature concerning the development of the funeral industry and burial. The second section presents a historic ethnography of the development of the green burial movement in the U.S. This is followed by a section examining the literature on green burial. In an effort to contextualize the green burial movement with reference to the larger environmental movement, the final section reviews literature on correlates of support for the environmental movement.

The Funeral Industry

American culture has perpetuated a death fearing and death denying attitude through funeral practices and even pop culture (Laddman 2000). This is the result of more than a century of funerary practices that have moved the social and physical role of the deceased further and further away from the living. This was most commonly accomplished by the introduction of the professionalized death care industry or the funeral director (Bartlett and Riches 2007).

History of Deathcare Work

The idea of observing or keeping watch over the dead during the time between death and burial is an ancient practice found in societies all over the world (Puckle 1926). Although specific reasons for this practice may have varied by society this practice served two practical purposes: it allowed for the hope that the deceased may return to consciousness, and in the event that the latter did not occur it allowed the family and friends, so recently accustomed to caring for the sick, to adjust to the new conditions that come about with death. Thus, "watching" of the dead became a recognized institution. In Christian practices this event was characterized by the offering of special prayers for the deceased at a time when the soul might be considered in need of the spiritual support. These gatherings of family and friends, in the actual presence of the body, would consist of prayer for the soul of the departed and the opportunity to console those afflicted by the loss. Puckle suggests that this practice is the origin of the "wake" or "watching." Other practices were more formalized and required the assistance of paid workers. These included the Jewish "Lykwake" (professional watcher), wailers, mutes and sin eaters, socially taking on the sins of the dead (Puckle 1926). Thus began the concept of a funeral as a production involving the coordination of workers, burial and feast (Reis 1991). The power and wealth that an individual possessed in life were reflected in the extravagance of his or her funeral in many parts of Latin America (Voekel 2002) including in parts of the American Southwest (Will de Chaparro 2007). In the Puritanical culture that is associated with American colonies lavish and emotion-laden funeral ceremonies were viewed as vulgar and were greatly discouraged (Hockey et. al 2001). However even among these societies it was customary to hand out funerary notices and special death cakes (Davies 2005) both of which were produced especially for such occasions. The emergence of these paid positions of death workers laid the ground work for the undertaker, a single individual who coordinated all aspects of the wake and burial. In earlier cultures this individual would arrange watchers, wailers, mutes and oversee preparations for the funeral feast (Davies, 2005). At the beginning of the nineteenth century the role of the undertaker shifted from that of a social event coordinator to one of a medicalized professional, but one still capable of pulling together all aspects of the funeral.

Modern Death

The contemporary relationship between society and death began during the "modernist era" of the nineteenth century. Advances in the fields of medicine and human anatomy characterized this time period of early modernity (Davies 2005). As industrialization began people moved from agrarian and family based living situations into cities and among strangers (Wirzba 2003). With this change came new meaning of death and burial. Moller (1996:25) paraphrases Weber in stating that "beaucratization of society removed many social functions from family and fellowship networks and place them in autonomous institutions that are independent of emotional ties." As this happens the role of formal caretakers of the dead emerges. At the same time concerns over burial space and close physical proximity to the living became an issue (Will de Chaparro 2007) fueled by increased medical understanding of bacteria and contamination (Sappol 2004). Interest in death and corpses was not limited to students in medical schools. "Popular anatomy" as it was referred to could be easily found in magazines and newspapers, and the wealthy would even acquire bodies to be dissected in their homes during parties (Moller 1996; Sappol 2004). Necrophilia became a common theme in popular literature (Davies 2005). Thus Moller argues that during this time frame the dead body was seen to have two important social values: a.) as a source of macabre eroticism and b.) as a means of furthering knowledge about life (Moller 1996, pg. 10). This "modernist" approach to death and dying was a drastic change from earlier agrarian ways. Berry (2003) writes that the difference between industrialism and agrarianism defines the most fundamental human difference and represents two very opposite ways of looking at ourselves, other creatures and the world. In the industrial worldview death was medicalized, eroticized and ultimately feared. In agrarian societies death was viewed as something respected, inevitable and simply part of the "circle of life" (Feagan 2007; Wirzba 2003). In this more accepting approach the dying were surrounded and supported by family and friends up until the final moment of death. The body would then be bathed and dressed by family members and laid out in the home for the community to come and pay their last respects while the local cabinetmaker would fashion a coffin using materials purchased from the local general store (Moller 1996). Burial would take place within a few days on a family plot or in a small community cemetery (Wirzba 2003) and would be followed by a gathering with food and drink to honor the dead. The agrarian acceptance of death came from earlier notions of the "good" or "tame' death (Moller 1996; Will de Chaparro 2007) that date back to the European Middle Ages. Here death and dying were characterized by tranquility and acceptance. Death was very much a communal and public act tied to very specific anticipated rituals surrounding mourning and the deathbed (Moller 1996). It was through these rituals that the dying individual was guaranteed a "good" death and, it was hoped, divine salvation (Davies 2005). Death in contemporary American society is overwhelmingly facilitated by the medical field, where the dying are removed from the public sphere and into specialized institutions: hospitals, nursing homes and hospices (Moller 1996). Upon death the deceased are completely removed from family and friends and placed in morgues to await the funeral directors, who will take complete charge over them until they are buried or cremated. This process occurs in a quick and well-organized manner (Moller 1996) often with consideration for easing the work of the embalmer in mind (Harvey 2001). Consequently we now live in a society in which when someone dies it is assumed that a funeral home will step in and take care of arrangements and the necessity of the "funeral package" including such things as embalming, makeup and carefully selected clothing, coffin, vault and even electronic memorials are not even questioned. This arrangement has considerable impact upon us as both consumers and in terms of maintaining social distance from death. In his dissertation on the funeral industry in Japan Hikaru Suzuki writes: The argument of the model is that the interactions among consumers, values, and industries are all responsible for the change, reproduction and continuation of cultural values and practices. People's satisfaction with products and services and their consumption patterns demonstrate current cultural values and practices. These values and the repetition of these practices lead to mass production and mass consumption, which in turn helps generate ranges of heterogeneous forms and shapes within an overall homogeneous cultural structure. Finally the commoditization of a product serves as an opportunity to mediate changes in a culture (Suzuki, 2001, p. 6). Suzuki is suggesting that the commodified product influences the needs and tastes of the consumer and not, as one might think, the other way around. In the funeral industry this means that the undertaker designates what products and services are needed, the need being a proper or respectable funeral- then sells these to the bereaved. Given that this is a profit driven and competitive industry the opportunity to create more and expensive funerary "needs" is inevitable. As the previous two sections illustrate, the vocation of the undertaker slowly came into being by unifying and monopolizing the services and resources considered necessary in order to produce an American funeral. In doing so the funeral industry has had a homogenizing effect on the cultural ceremony of the funeral, turning from a simple ritual consisting of the removal of the deceased from the living society to a consumable product that has jaded societal attitudes towards death and dying. If Suzuki's argument holds, then the same mechanisms that led us to these current practices can just as easily reintegrate death into society by way of "products" such as green burial. Minimizing the social distance between individuals and death may aid in diminishing the fear society bears towards death, thus, allowing for a new relationship between attitudes and perceptions of death and society to emerge.

Historic Ethnography

To better understand the green burial movement as a social phenomenon this section presents a brief ethnography of some of the pioneers of the movement in the U.S. Each of these individuals has demonstrated great passion and dedication to their work in the field of death care, environmental conservation and green burial. For these four individuals the path to work in this field has been a combination of unique experiences both professionally and personally.

Dr. William Campbell - Memorial Ecosystems and Founder of Ramsey Creek Preserve

Dr. William (Billy) Campbell, MD, founder of Ramsey Creek Preserve, was born and raised in the foothills of western South Carolina's mountains. As a child growing up he took great interest in spending time in the woods and fields that surrounded his family farm outside of Westminster. In 1977 he graduated from Emory University with a B. S. in Biology and in 1981 from the Medical University of South Carolina with his M.D. In 1984 he returned home to Westminster to practice medicine and has been the town's only physician since 1994.

Campbell's interest in natural burial began with an 8th grade teacher who shared with the class his desire to be buried in a burlap bag and have a tree planted over him. At Emory he became interested in death studies after reading Jessica Mitford's *The American Way of Death* and Ernest Becker's *The Denial of Death.* In medical school Campbell attributed his growing interest in death care to spending many hours in a room full of cadavers. After reading a medical anthropology text that included a description of New Guinea "spirit forests" he had the idea of creating a new type of memorial park that would both conserve land and provide space for burial. After the unexpected death of his father in 1985, Campbell, his brother and his brother in-law took care of funeral and burial arrangements. The experience left him unsatisfied, as he felt that the funeral homes take advantage of people's grief in order to sell them expensive and seemingly unnecessary services. This strengthened his conviction of the importance of conservation burial and his desire to pursue a career in this field. He spent the next 10 years speaking about death care as a tool for conservation, then in 1996 Campbell and his wife Kimberley founded Memorial Ecosystems. Finally, in 1998 Billy Campbell's dream became a reality when he opened Ramsey Creek Preserve, the first green burial preserve in the United States, in South Carolina. Everything that goes into the earth at the preserve is carefully restricted. Only native trees and flowers are allowed. Bodies are placed in the earth un-embalmed in plain, pine caskets or biodegradable burial shrouds. Simple stones mark gravesites. For long term tracking GPS technology is utilized to distinguish individual burial locations.

Joe Shehee - Director, Green Burial Council

To strengthen the alternative burial movement the Green Burial Council was established in 1995 by ecological design pioneer Joe Shehee, a former Jesuit lay minister who had previously done strategic communications work for the cemetery and funeral industries. In addition to this work, Shehee has been involved in social advocacy. Like Campbell, he desired to pursue an endeavor of his own making. In following with this mission Shehee and his family moved just outside of Joshua Tree National Park in California. His plan was to build an ecological retreat named "The Pilgrimage," a place where people could seek solace in the barren terrain. For two years Shehee oversaw the building of the retreat. During that time he lost interest in the project and became more concerned with the landscape itself as an endangered resource and one that he wanted to work to preserve. He had thought that the move to California would distance him from death care, though the opposite proved to be true. Working on "The Pilgrimage" and isolated from urban life Shehee took notice of things that he was previously unaware of. In the April 2008 edition of the American Funeral Director, he is quoted as stating of this experience, "I saw how much life and death are intertwined in nature. And I wondered why so much of conventional death care seems so devoid of life-especially cemeteries.

There are coiffed grounds but nothing natural." With the support of his wife Shehee sold their home and used the money to establish the Green Burial Council in 2005. The mission of this organization is to promote ethical and environmentally sustainable death care practices. It is Shehee's intention that the council will help people see the burial process as a means of assisting in the restoration and preservation of natural areas. The Green Burial Council works closely with other conservation and environmental groups, including Memorial Ecosystems and Eternal Reefs, to promote and educate on natural burial practices to both the consumer and funeral directors. One of the Council's most important initiatives has been its approval of funeral homes that offer a Green Burial Package, an idea that came from Thomas Lynch, owner of Lynch and Sons Funeral Directors in Michigan. The intent is for funeral homes to offer environmentally-conscious consumers a "green" alternative to the traditional burial package. Through this endeavor the Council has been able to work closely with funeral directors in developing different techniques for preparing and presenting bodies without formaldehyde-based embalming fluids or other chemicals.

Don Brawley - Founder of Eternal Reefs

In May of 1998 Eternal Reefs cast its first memorial reef into the ocean off of the Florida Keys. The idea behind this organization began not as a burial alternative but as a solution to an environmental problem. While in college in the late 1980's founder Don Brawley and his roommate spent their breaks diving in the Florida Keys and over the years took notice of the deterioration and degradation of the reefs. After graduating from college Brawley wanted to contribute to the restoration and protection of the fragile reef eco system. Thus the concept of the reef ball was born utilizing material that would replicate the natural marine environment and attract marine life. In 1990 the Reef Ball Development Group and the Reef Ball Foundation completed the first reef ball project near Ft. Lauderdale. Since that time over 3,500 similar projects have been launched around the world, placing over 400,000 reef balls on the ocean floor. In 1998 Carleton Glen Palmer, Don Brawley's father-in-law, told Brawley that when he died he wanted to have his cremated remains put into a reef and released into the ocean. Shortly after he made this request, Palmer died and on May 1,1998 Brawley honored his request by launching a reef ball bearing Palmer's remains off of Saratosa. In the historic background, posted on the organizations website, Brawley wrote that Palmer made this request because, "he (Palmer) couldn't think of a more beautiful place to be laid to rest." A short time after Palmer's memorial service, Brawley was reflecting on his father-in-laws final wish and realized that if one person felt this way about the reefs, others may as well. Locally, he began advertising the reef balls as an option for laying to rest cremated remains. As the memorial reefs gained popularity in the area, Brawley decided to expand advertising and develop a website, giving the organization the name *Eternal Reefs* and expanding services to include allowing family and friends to assist in the making of reef balls and accommodations for memorial services and "reef drops." Realistically, memorial reefs are not a truly green alternative. The process of cremation emits harmful toxins into the air and some people elect to be embalmed before their bodies are cremated. Fossil fuels are burned in the transportation process of getting the remains to Florida and in the boats taken out to drop the reef. I decided to include *Eternal Reefs* in the discussion for this thesis, regardless of this, for two reasons; first, because it still represents an alternative to traditional burial and support for one type of burial alternative may indicate a willingness to support another type of alternative. Secondly, this type of memorialization still requires the use of fewer natural resources than ground burial. The materials used to make the reef balls are non-toxic and completely environmentally friendly and environmentally restorative. Thus I concluded that this organization promotes a "greener" alternative to a traditional burial and therefore merited inclusion.

Jerrigrace Lyons - Founder/Director of Final Passages and Death Midwife

Jerrigrace Lyons is included in this ethnography because she is the founder and director of an organization that promotes and facilitates green burial and because her work represents the polar opposite of the traditional American funeral and the extreme example of natural burial. Lyons' background is in the field of spiritual healing. She is a reiki master and Trager practitioner. She became involved in death care work when her long time friend and reiki mentor Carolyn Whiting died unexpectedly. Whiting had left specific instructions about how to care for her body postmortem; no embalming, no autopsy, no mortuary- she requested that loved ones bathe and dress her body and then prepare an intimate home memorial. She asked that her ashes be scattered around the world on her friends' travels. Lyons was involved in this entire process and it was this profound experience that motivated her to found Final Passages and begin a career as a death midwife. Based in California, Final Passages is a nonprofit organization that seeks to educate people about funeral and burial options. In addition to this mission they also offer the services of death midwives to individuals who elect to care for their deceased on their own. These death midwives assist with paperwork and obtaining any necessary permits, facilitate transportation and the care of a body for a home wake or funeral. Lyons believes that home wakes are meaningful rituals that help people let go of their fears surrounding death and dying. Clients of Final Passages have even suggested that washing and dressing the body of their recently deceased loved one has even allowed them to come to terms with the reality of their death in a way that would not have been possible in a funeral home. Death midwives are trained in workshops run by Final Passages that educate on at home death care including such practical matters as the cleaning of the body, anointing with scented waters or oils, the particulars of rigor mortis and proper positioning of dry ice under the organs of the deceased. This is also the students' opportunity to become familiar with the death midwife's tools of the trade; medical gloves, adult diapers, nail clippers, alcohol, dry shampoo, make-up, music, essential oils, x-acto knives, suturing kits and Krazy Glue (Strubbe 2007).

Susanne Wiigh-Masak - Head ofPromessa Organic AB-Sweden

Wiigh-Masak is a biologist and engineer from Lars, Sweden who has developed what is perhaps the ultimate green burial option and cremation alternative-promession. While cremation gained popularity for providing a solution to the amount of land used up in traditional burial it has not been considered an ecologically sound alternative due to the release of toxins, such as mercury from dental fillings, into the environment as the body is burned. In the process of promession bodies are not burned but placed in a biodegradable casket and placed in liquid nitrogen and frozen to 196 degrees Celsius. This process makes the body very brittle. It is then shaken until it disintegrates into a powder. All non-biodegradable parts, such as fillings or prosthetics, are removed by machinery. The "premains" are then placed in coffins made from maize or potato starch and are returned to the family for burial. A tree is planted over the burial site and it is nourished by both coffin and remains. The remains are fully absorbed into the earth within about a year. The concept of promession has been a twenty year endeavor for Wiigh-Masak. It stemmed from a desire to engineer a means of body disposal that would be advantageous to the earth. As a biologist, Wiigh-Masak has studied and lectured on the environmental aspects of the cycle of life and processes of mulching, burning and rotting. She was intrigued by the fact that other types of organic matter returns to the earth and contribute to the cycle; but this was typically not the case with human remains- traditional burial promotes the rot of a body and cremation renders it unable to be absorbed into the earth. This understanding of the difference between decomposition and rotting fueled her research into a burial alternative. In an interview with the Daily Undertaker (McNally 2007), Wiigh-Masak points out that decomposition requires the same conditions that sustain life; air, proper moisture and proper temperature. If the correct conditions are in place it allows the substance to break down to the nutrient level that can sustain the earth. The opposite, rot, occurs when remains are too large for air and soil to break it down in a positive manner. For this reason she contends that promession is more environmentally sound than green or natural burial in a shroud. Since her youth, Wiigh-Masak has had a great interest in science and gardening, especially in composting. This interest in science led her to pursue a degree in marine biology at the University of Gothenburg. After graduating she and her husband started a clam business in addition to a vegetable business that furthered her research in composting and would eventually lead to the work that started Promessa Organic AB Currently, only two countries, Sweden and South Korea, have operating "promatoriums," facilities that do promession. Others, including the U.S. and the U.K., are looking into making promession possible as well. Should this process become available for consumer consumption in the US it would have a tremendous impact on the green burial movement, as it would not only offer an additional burial alternative but it would also make other alternatives, such as memorial reefs, more ecologically sound.

Each of these five individuals represent a distinct vein in the US (and global)

Green Burial movement. Others have also contributed to the development of this movement. While their work has been instrumental in the success that it has seen thus far, I selected these five as pioneers of the movement not only because some were among the first to advocate for green burial in the US, but also because they represent the full variety of options that green burial has to offer. Utilizing their various backgrounds they have worked both individually and collectively to promote more environmentally friendly means of burial with the intention of saving the environment and as an opportunity to provide a more meaningful way of burying or memorializing a deceased loved one.

Green Burial

Much of the previous research on the green burial movement has examined the detrimental relationship between traditional means of burial and the environment (Feagan 2007; Kaufman 1998; McCausland 2008; Stowe et al 2001). The research concludes that the effects have been immense. Virtually no mention of burial alternatives has been offered nor is the relationship between burial and attitudes towards death considered. In his book *A Brief History of Death,* Davies states that "the implication of the shifting meaning of death in ecological ethics and consumerist individualism could be described in terms of ecological immortality; as the issue of waste disposal became a greater concern of ordinary life it should not come as a surprise that the disposal of the human body should also come to be seen as part of the same general problem" (2005; pg 86). Is American society prepared to view burial with such an ethos of waste? Could this movement represent enough of a shift in structure and values to change the way we approach the business of funerals and the act of dying? The funeral home industry generates $20 billion dollars a year (Stubbe 2007) and it is certainly in their best interest to keep Americans consuming traditional funeral packages. There may always be a need for funeral providers, as involvement in burial ceremonies aids the bereaved in coming to terms with the death of their loved one and initiates the mourning process. Funerals and other ceremonies provide a meaningful way for people to act out their feelings and to provide security, identity and confidence (Stowe, Schmidt and Green 2001). Suzuki (2001) found that in Japanese culture commercial funerals and the highly bureaucratic manner in which they treat death decreased fear of death and dying.

Support for Environmental Movements

As previously stated the green burial movement is part of the large environmental movement. This is due to the large organizational base and staying power that environmentalism possesses (Mertig and Dunlap 2001). In addition to this, it has been noted that the movement has significant institutional and cultural effects within most industrialized nations and beyond (Buttel 1992; Dalton 1994). Scott (1990) noted that of all contemporary social movements, environmentalism is often considered the one with the greatest level of actual and potential public support and represents significant ideological challenges to the status quo (Mertig and Dunlap 2001). Further potential indicators of support for the movement will be discussed in the following section.

Income and Education

Information on socioeconomic status is widely varied. While some studies of industrialized countries seem to conclude that the environmental movement derives its fundamental support from the middle class which are typically more highly educated, employed in public services and have incomes in the medium range (Cotgrove and Duff 1980; Eckersley 1989; Kriesi 1989; and Morrison and Dunlap 1986) others have concluded that individuals with lower levels of education and income are more likely than others to demonstrate concern for the environment given that they are more likely to have immediate experiences with environmental pollution (Nas and Dekker 1996). Rohrschneider (1988, 1990) concluded that positive attitudes toward the environment can be explained by both general value orientations ('symbolic politics approach') and sociotropic evaluations of the state of the environment.

Regional and Urban/Rural Differences

Support for environmentalism in the U.S. generally varies by where one lives.

Previous research that focused on the social bases of environmentalism in the U.S. has found that urban residents are more concerned about the environment than rural residents (Bennett and McBeth 1998). These rural-urban differences in support were thought to be especially high in the West, where extractive-based employment is high. However Jones et al. (1999) found these differences were not as pronounced and anticipated that they would further diminish as the dependency on the extractive-based sector of the economy declines. Further they found that while support of environmentalism was high in the West support for and knowledge of it was growing in other regions of the country such as in the Appalachian mountain region. In examining the planning and development of waterfronts in Portland, Oregon, Hagerman (2007) found support for environmental movements to be especially high in the West. Brown (2006) also found support for environmental movements to be strong in the West. This research suggests that there is evidence that suggests that support for environmentalism is greatest in the West.

Race

The issue of race is relatively well studied in literature based on environmental quality. Typically this research is primarily focused on environmental injustice. Hines (2007) found that African Americans were disproportionally exposed to pollution from chemical plants. Racial minorities demonstrate high levels of environmental concern when negatively impacted by pollution and waste (Bullard 2007; Collins and Doolittle 2006). Communities affected by such injustices have employed various techniques such as grassroots coalitions and community based networking to combat environmental injustices (Hines 2007). Based on this research it is reasonable to conclude that there are differences in support for environmentalism based on race.

Gender

The research suggests that women are generally more concerned than men about the environment. Studies tend to find that women express greater concern over potential environmental risks (Blocker and Eckberg 1989; Davidson and Freudenburg 1996; McStay and Dunlap 1983) Many argue that women are generally more concerned about environmental issues that men (Davidson and Freudenburg 1996; Van Liere and Dunlap 1980). This tends to be the case for a variety of social, cultural, structural and biological reasons (Tindall, Davies and Mauboules 2003). It is suggested that since women do more nurturing and caring work they are socialized to value cooperation and concern for others (Davidson and Freudenburg 1996; Mohai 1992; Van Liere and Dunlap 1980).

CHAPTER III
METHODOLOGY

This chapter describes the data and the data collection. Research questions utilized for this study are given. The dependent and independent variables are introduced and discussed. Finally, the data analysis is described and limitations are presented.

Data and Sample

Data collected from the 2007 American Association of Retired People (AARP) Funeral and Burial Planners survey are used for this analysis. The data are representative of the U.S. population of adults 50 and older and includes both AARP members and nonmembers. The survey is part of an ongoing AARP research project that studies funeral and burial plan decisions of 50+ Americans. This particular year was selected for use because it is the first time information on alternative burial was collected for this survey and it is the only national survey that addresses the topic. International Communications Research of Media, Pennsylvania conducted the survey in May of 2007 over a ten-day period. The data were collected via telephone interviews using a fully replicated, stratified, single-stage random-digit dialing sample of telephone households. Both AARP members and non-members were targeted for the sample population. The data were provided by the AARP Office of Knowledge Management. The total sample size is 1,089.

Variables

Dependent Variable

The dependent variable is support for green burial. The data are based on responses to the following question:

1.) "How interested would you be in having a burial that is more environmentally friendly?" (FB-17) Five response categories were presented in Likert-scale format for the question. Response categories ranged from the following: "very interested," "somewhat interested," "neutral," "not very interested," and "not interested at all." This variable was collapsed and recoded to into two response categories: those who would favor a more environmentally friendly burial (recoded as "1") and those who would not (recoded as "3").

Independent Variables

In this study, the independent variables are region, income, highest level of education, and gender. Region is a nominal-level variable with 4 response categories of "Northeast region," "North Central region," "South region" and "West region." Income is an ordinal-level variable with 14 response categories. Of these 14 categories two were not mutually exclusive. These two were labeled "missing" and excluded from the analysis. Education is an ordinal-level variable with the following six response categories; "less than high school graduate," "high school graduate or GED certificate," "technical, trade or business school," "some college or university work," "college or university graduate," or "post graduate or professional schooling after college degree." Sex is a nominal-level variable with the categories of "male" and "female. Age is an ordinal-level variable that was originally as an open ended question in which respondents were asked to provide their age. Response categories of "refused" and "I don't know" were also provided. This resulted in a range of 50 to 91 years. I collapsed this data into the following age groupings; "50-59 years", "60-69 years", "70-79 years", "80-89 years" and "90+."

Research Questions

1. Does support for green burial vary by geographic region?
2. What is the relationship between income and support for green burial?
3. What is the effect of education on support for green burial?
4. What is the effect of age on support for green burial?

Data Analysis

I ran frequencies on each of the six items representing the independent variables and the one representing the dependent variable to insure that the data were clean. After doing so I recoded AGE into a new variable (RAGE) to result in fewer response categories. INCOME was also recoded and two response categories, "$50,000 and over' and "$50,000 and under" were labeled as missing. I removed these categories because they were not mutually exclusive. This resulted in 112 cases labeled as missing for this variable. The item representing the dependent variable (FUNE) was also recoded (to R2FUNE) into a variable with only two response categories (those who would elect a green burial and those who would not). After running a descriptive analysis, I ran Pearson's correlations and chi square on all of the variables in the analysis. Results for both descriptive analysis and correlation matrices are presented in chapter four.

Limitations

There are several limitations within this research project. The primary limitation is the lack of previous data from which to draw comparisons or conduct a longitudinal study. As stated in the previous chapter, as there is a lack of literature available on green burial I had to rely on research on environmentalism in general to support the effects of the independent variables. The question representing the dependent variable, support for green burial, is not an exact measure of support and is simply a proxy for this variable. Two separate independent variables, income and education are used in place of the one variable socioeconomic status because the data lacks information on occupation, typically an important factor when calculating SES. However, it is important to note that given that this particular target population is either retired or nearing retirement and therefore questions on occupation were not included. An additional limitation is that only adults over age

50 were surveyed. Thus information on younger adults is lacking. This is an especially important component given that the research shows that in looking at support for environmentalism, younger individuals show more support than their older counterparts. It would have been beneficial to this research if data were available on younger Americans as well. However, it is possible that there is a benefit to looking at this particular population as oppose to the younger generations. This older population is targeted for this type of research because they are more likely to be thinking about or actively planning burial arrangements for themselves, spouses or parents. Also it should be noted that support for the movement and actually carrying out these types of burial plans are entirely different. An additional complexity presented in these circumstances is that the issue at hand is ultimately death, and the younger portion of the population is less likely to invest much time contemplating their own mortality (Kearl, 2009). Therefore, in spite of the initial limitations presented by this variable I decided to include it in this analysis.

CHAPTER IV
RESULTS

The following chapter includes a descriptive analysis and presents findings from the bivariate analysis. The four research questions are discussed.

Characteristics of Respondents

Table 1 displays a descriptive analysis of the dependent and independent variables. The average age for respondents was almost 61 years (60.9 years). There were significantly more younger respondents than older ones, as 44.6% were in the 50-59 age category. Due to the nature of mortality these numbers are acceptable and reflective of the larger U.S. population. In actual age, the youngest respondent was 50 and the oldest 95. There were slightly more females (54%) than males (46%). The majority of respondents were white (75%) and reported living in the South Region (39%). Most respondents (55.5%) reported having graduated from high school or having some college education (36% and 19% respectively). Approximately 32% of the respondents reported an annual income between $30,000 and $75,000.

Table 1
Characteristics of Respondents

Variable	N	%
Gender		
Male	501	46.1
Female	586	53.9
Age		
50-59	485	44.6
60-69	316	29.1
70-79	188	17.3
80-89	84	7.7
90-95	14	1.3
Race*		
White	816	75.1
Black	103	9.5
Other	57	5.3
Refused	30	2.8
Income*		
<$ 10,000	80	8.9
$10,000-$15,000	76	7.0
$15,000-$20,000	67	6.2
$20,000-$25,000	53	4.9
$25,000-$30,000	42	3.7
$30,000-$40,000	111	10.2
$40,000-$50,000	75	6.8
$50,000-$75,000	104	9.6
$75,000-$100,000	77	7.1
>$ 100,000	96	8.8
Don't Know	30	2.8
Refused	135	7.9

Table 1 cont.
Characteristics of Respondents

Variable	N	%
Education*		
<High School	195	17.9
High School Graduate	396	36.4
Some College	206	19
College Graduate	131	12.1
Graduate School or More	105	9.6
Technical School/Other	32	3
Refused	22	2
Geographic Region (U.S.)		
Northeast	189	17.4
North Central	268	24.7
South	421	38.7
West	209	19.2

Note. N= 1,087. Source: AARP Funeral and Burial Planners Survey (2007)
Totals do not equal 100% due to missing cases

Research Questions

The following section addresses results in relation to the original research questions presented in the previous chapter.

Question 1

What is the relationship between support for green burial and geographic region?

I expected to find a difference in support for green burial by geographic region.

Specifically, I expected that support would be greatest in the West since Brown (2006) and Hagerman (2007) found that participation and support for environmentalism was greatest in the West. The data were not consistent with these findings. As shown in table 2 the majority of supporters for green burial came from the South 32% followed by the West at 23%. The chi-square test equals 6.708. This suggests a relatively insignificant relationship between region and support for green burial.

Table 2
Support for Green Burial by Geographic Region

Region	Yes N	Yes %	No N	No %	Total
Northeast	45	19.7	144	16.7	189
North Central	57	25	212	24.7	269
South	73	32	348	40.5	421
West	53	23.2	156	18.1	209
All Regions	228	100	860	100	1088*

Note. $X2=6.708$. $df=3$. $p<.1$
Total does not equal to 1089 due to missing cases

Question 2
What is the relationship between income and support for green burial? Table 4 presents the data on income. I expected to find that middle to higher levels of education and middle to lower levels of income would correlate with greater support of green burial. 42% of supporters of green burial made over $50,000 per year and 58% of supporters made less than this amount annually. The findings

from the literature on support for environmentalism and SES varied greatly. Cotgrove and Duff (1980), Morrison and Dunlap (1986), Kriesi (1989) and Eckersley (1989) all found that in industrialized nations support for environmentalism was greatest among individuals with middle to higher levels of SES. However my findings are more in agreement with the work of Nas and Dekker (1996) who found support to be greatest among individuals with lower SES. The chi-squared statistic is 22.609. This suggests a relatively significant relationship between income and support for green burial.

Table 3
Support for Green Burial and Income

Income	YES N	YES %	NO N	NO %	Total
LT $10,000	14	7.4	66	8.8	80
$10,000 LT $15,000	16	8.5	60	7.9	76
$15,000 LT $20,000	12	6.4	55	7.2	67
$20,000 LT $25,000	11	5.9	42	5.5	53
$25,000 LT $30,000	10	5.3	32	4.2	42
$30,000 LT $40,000	20	10.6	90	11.8	110
$40,000 LT $50,000	12	6.4	63	8.3	75
$50,000 Lt $75,000	32	17	72	9.5	104
$75,000 LT $100,000	25	13.3	52	6.8	77
$100,000 or more	22	11.7	74	9.6	96
Don't Know	9	4.8	21	2.8	47
Refuse	5	2.7	134	17.6	139
Total	188	100*	761	100*	949*

Note. $X^2= 22.609$ $df= 11$ $P<.05$
"Total does not equal 1089 due to missing cases.
**Totals do not equal 100% due to missing cases

Question 3

What is the effect of education on support for green burial? Level of education did have a relationship with level of support for green burial. Table presents data on this variable. Contrary to what I expected, I found that those who reported lower levels of education were more likely to support green burial. In fact level of support was found to be highest (35%) among those who reported that their highest level of education was a high school diploma. As education increased support began to decrease. This supports the idea that the movement is perceived as a grassroots effort with interest coming from the middle class. The data also supports part of the literature on SES and support for environmental movements. Specifically, Nas and Dekker (1996) found that individuals with lower incomes and lower levels of education were more likely to be supportive of environmentalism as they were more likely to be negatively impacted by environmental contamination. The chi-squared statistic is 18.858. This suggests a relatively significant relationship between education and support for green burial.

Table 4
Support for Green Burial and Education

| | YES | | NO | | |
Highest level of Education	N	%	N	%	Total
Less than HS Grad	26	11.4	169	19.7	195
HS Grad	79	34.6	317	80.0	396
Some College	44	19.3	162	18.9	206
Graduated College	39	17.1	92	10.7	131
Graduate School or More	31	13.6	73	8.5	105
Technical School/Other	5	2.2	28	3.3	33
Refused	4	1.8	17	2.0	21
Total	228	100*	858	100*	1086*

$X2=18.858$ df^6 $p< .005$
*total not equal to 1089 due to missing cases
**totals not equal to 100% due to missing cases

Question 4

What is the effect of age on support of green burial? Even though the question of age presented unique circumstance given the limitations of the sample, I expected that greater levels of support would be associated with younger respondents. Of the oldest age bracket (90-95) support for green burial was less than 1%. As I had anticipated, support was greatest among the youngest age group, 50-59 year olds, at 57%. Support steadily decreases as age of respondents increases. This corresponds with previous research which suggests that support for environmental movements decreases with age. It is also possible that older participants do not state willingness to consider green burial because there may be a correlation between advanced age and preplanning of burial arrangements. As such, it is possible that these individuals are not considering green burial because they already have burial arrangements in place and perhaps already paid for. The chi-squared statistic is 19.650. This suggests a relatively significant relationship between age and support for green burial.

Table 5
Support for Green Burial and Age

Age	YES N	%	NO N	%	Total
50-59	130	56.5	355	41.3	485
60-69	59	25.7	258	30	317
70-79	30	13	159	18.5	189
80-89	10	4.3	74	8.6	84
90-95	1	.4	13	1.5	14

X^2= 19.650 df=4 p<.001

Summary

Bivariate analyses were used to identify characteristics of supporters of green burial. The intent was to examine the possibility that gender, education, income and/or age may have an impact on level of support for this newly emerging movement in the U.S. In theory, individuals possessing certain characteristics within these four variables would express varying levels of support for green burial based on those sociodemographic attributes. Basic descriptive analysis revealed that the majority of the sample consisted of individuals who were white, living in the south, had some college experience and where somewhere in the 60-69 age range. Approximately equal numbers of women and men were surveyed. Findings show that support did vary based on conditions of the independent variables. Perhaps the most interesting finding was the effect of education. Support was greatest among individuals who reported their highest level of education as being either a high school diploma or some college. Educational attainment beyond and below this was correlated with a decrease in support. Further analysis would be necessary to rule out the influence of any other variables on this relationship. The results from the analysis of region were unexpected and contrary to the literature. One possibility is that defining parameters of region could vary from those used by International Communications Research for this survey. There is also the possibility that supporters of green burial simply vary from supporters of other types of environmentalism.

CHAPTER V
DISCUSSION

The following chapter discusses the results from the previous chapter and the implications of these results for the green burial movement in general. This chapter also presents a discussion of the cultural implications of the movement and the strained relationship between death and society.

Supporters of Green Burial

It was my intention to use data results discussed in the previous chapter to learn more about who supports this new movement and what are shared characteristics of these supporters. Based on the AARP survey data the average supporter was young, for the sample this meant that they fell in the 50-59 age range however based on the finding and those found in the literature we can assume that younger Americans are more likely to support this cause. Whether or not this support translates into the later decision to elect this burial option is a subject for future research. Supporters are more likely to be women than men. This finding was consistent with the research that women are more likely than men to express concern over potential environmental risks (Blocker and Eckberg 1989; Davidson and Freudenburg 1996; McStay and Dunlap 1983) and that they are more likely than men to be concerned with environmental issues (Davidson and Freudenburg 1996; Van Liere and Dunlap 1980). It has been suggested that since women do more nurturing and caring work they are socialized to value cooperation and concern for others (Van Liere and Dunlap 1980; Mohai 1992; Davidson and Freudenburg 1996). Additionally, data from the survey shows that women were almost twice as likely as men to preplan burial arrangements for themselves or someone else. This involvement in preparing burial arrangements may also mean that women are more likely than men to have heard of green burial and therefore are more open to consider this option. On average, supporters were more likely to be living in the South than in any other region. This was an unexpected finding since the literature indicated that participation in environmentalism was found to be especially high in West states (Brown 2006; Hagerman 2007). One possible explanation for this inconsistency with the literature higher level of support for green burial in this region may be a result of accessibility. Of the thirteen operating green cemeteries in the U.S. five are located in the South and one more is in the process of development (The Center for Natural Burial). It is possible that individuals living in the South are more likely to have heard of these options and, are in turn more likely to consider them. Close physical proximity to a green cemetery is especially imperative to those choosing burial alternative as a means of reducing negative impact on the environment. For these individuals shipping a body or cremated remains two or three states away for burial would have the same negative implications as utilizing a traditional cemetery. On average the majority of green burial supporters earned less than $50,000 a year and did not have high levels of education. Nas and Dekker (1996) found that individuals with lower levels of education and income are more likely than others to demonstrate concern for the environment given that they are more likely to have immediate experiences with environmental pollution. Income may also be an important variable in the decision to elect green burial if the reason behind this decision was economic. As green burial becomes more prevalent, individuals who are unable or unwilling to afford traditional services may begin to utilize this option as a means of cheaper burial. Although prices vary by location and options such as reef balls are more costly, the average green burial is still thousands of dollars less than a traditional funeral. Future research is needed to understand if environmental or economic reasons are the primary motive behind the decision to elect a green burial.

Death as a Variable

Overall the findings from the AARP survey were fairly consistent with findings from previous research on support for environmental movements. However, there is one significant difference between this and previous studies. The emphasis in environmentalism is to sustain and protect the environment. Typically individuals who participate in these movements gain a sense that they are protecting the earth, and that by doing their part they will be agents of change and renewal of life on the earth. There is a focus on life. Living it, sustaining it and passing it on to the next generation. The idea of green burial is to accomplish the same end, though its adherents will not be around to enjoy the fruits of their own labor. At its core this movement is about burial and ultimately about death. Death remains a subject that is considered taboo in modern society and calls to mind images of rot and disease. As advances in medicine provide new opportunities for prevention and treatment, death becomes aligned with a failure to sustain life. In this context incorporating burial into the environmental movement seems like a paradox. At the same time it is not. There was a time when the ideology of death promoted it as a natural part of the life cycle, as something neither good nor bad but a neutral constant in everyone's life. As a movement green burial is attempting to reconstruct this ideology in a very physical sense to reintegrate the human body back into this system. While a growing number of Americans are willing to reuse and recycle, fewer may be willing to put these principles into practice with their own bodies. It is possible that any differences in support found in this data and in the literature could be attributed to societal attitudes towards death. I argue that in order to gain the fullest understanding of support of this movement a research tool should be constructed that considers attitudes towards death as a variable.

Environmentalism, Death and the 'Ethos of Waste'

Environmentalism is based, in part, on the premise of an obligation that we as human beings have to protect and sustain the earth. As a result of this obligation individuals are often forced to reconsider the way that they use and dispose of material resources. The relationship between humanity and garbage has developed an 'ethos of waste' which dictates how we view and relate to our material waste. Of this Guy Hawkins (2006) writes "modernity brought values such as convenience, cleanliness and replace ability, fostering the creation of an 'ethos of disposability' in which distance and denial pervaded out relationship with waste." Here again modernity has changed the social context of a relationship society has created with an outside force. This idea of object permanence, or the lack thereof birthed from the idea of replaceability, proved to be especially advantageous to the undertaker. Citing health concerns and the spread of contamination (Sappol 2002) acquired through knowledge gained as "medically trained" individuals, undertakers were able utilize this 'ethos of disposability' to break away from more environmentally conservative practices such as reusing coffins (for purposes of the wake) or multiple individuals in one grave (Davies 2005) in favor of single use vessels and burial plots. Initially this would have been well received; it was in line with newly emerging ideals about cleanliness and may have provided additional profit for coffin makers, grave diggers and other death workers. As the trade evolved from undertaker to funeral director so did the nature of the services he provided. What was once a simpler process of washing, embalming and dressing a corpse for burial in a pine box became an elaborate ceremony involving formaldehyde, cosmetics and specially designed clothing for the dead (Mitford 1963). Great time and effort went into preparing the body of the deceased and in making them appear "dignified," "serene," or "peacefully sleeping" rather than dead. Ironically these efforts were put, quite literally to waste, as the final destination of the body was placement in a vaulted casket to be deposited into the ground at burial. The impact of green burial on this 'ethos of waste' is twofold. First, it forces our society to consider the amount of waste we produce. Broto (2007) suggests that waste represents a central contradiction in our society: it represents that which we reject, yet we produce a great deal of it through our "inherently wasteful consumer lifestyles." Evidence of the waste we produce surrounds us. Hawkins (2006) writes that materiality makes waste denial impossible; waste asserts itself in our environment. He continues by stating that once we stop denying waste we begin to see it for its possibilities beyond just "rubbish." By doing so we can improve our relationship with waste. Overall environmentalism has done well addressing this issue with a wealth of research devoted to the negative impact that traditional burial has on the environment and looking very specifically at the amount of natural resources buried back in American cemeteries each year. The second part of this impact is not as well addressed perhaps in part because it is not as palatable to society. The relationship between green burial and the 'ethos of waste' forces individuals to consider a most difficult reality: once life has departed, the human body itself becomes material waste. If a particular corpse is embalmed, placed in a casket and then sealed in a vault the body is not allowed to decompose naturally thus circumventing the whole concept of "ashes to ashes." As such the image of cemeteries serving as quiet beacons of eternal rest becomes one of quasi landfills of chemically processed human remains. Being able to look at the body in this way would be difficult for some and even insulting or sacrilegious for others. This plays into society's desire to disassociate itself from anything pertaining to death. It also could be seen as damaging to the ego to see the physical manifestation of oneself (the body) reduced to material waste at death. However if as a society we are able to overcome this and see the body in this context this would better position us to make burial decisions that are more environmentally sound and, as adherents would argue, a more dignified alternative for the deceased.

Death and Culture in America: Overcoming the Social Distance

Through the rise of modernity, with its advances in medicine and sanitation and in conjunction with the changing of etiquette and social norms born from the Victorian era, the presence of death in American society had all but disappeared. This was mainly accomplished in two ways, by the removal of the dying into institutions such as hospitals, nursing homes and hospices (Moller 1996) and by the emergence of professional death workers such as the undertaker (Davies 2005). Doing this reduced societal contact with the deceased and reinforced beliefs that corpses were sources of contamination and disease (Sappol 2002) and therefore should be given over to the care of professionals. While the practice of embalming became widely utilized during the Civil War to preserve the bodies of Union soldiers for the journey home (Moller 1996), the popularity of the custom spread among the American general public by the early twentieth century (Laderman 2003). In its infancy embalming was typically done in the home of the deceased (Davies 2005) and wakes were held in a front room of the house, or the "parlor" (Puckle 1925). Family members and other loved ones would still have had the opportunity to be involved in the dressing or washing of the body and would have stayed with them during the visitation and remained so until the time of burial. As the physical space in which dying occurred shifted from the home into institutions so did the role of the undertaker. Before this shift he primarily aided the family in preparing the body for burial. However, after this role began to shift and he became more and more responsible for the deceased: embalming, washing dressing and even housing them in the funeral parlor until burial with increasingly less participation from the deceased's family. In today's society contact with the deceased has been minimized to virtually nothing; at the time of death or shortly thereafter to sign the body over to the funeral director and at the wake or burial. Hospitals have morgues where the deceased can wait for the funeral home staff discreetly hidden away from the living and wakes can be conducted with a closed coffin. The growing availability of e-condolences, accessible through funeral and newspaper websites, and online florists has created an environment in which even attendance at a funeral becomes optional and the living are completely alienated from this social ritual surrounding death. The occupation of the funeral director was formally established to address the perceived need to remove the care of the dead from the public sector for health and etiquette reasons. Death and death work has been considered socially taboo throughout the ages and would have been especially distasteful to the delicate sensibilities of modern, civilized individuals. Historically other death workers such as mutes, wailers, sin eaters and watchers were considered social outcasts who were only called upon when their services were needed. In the dawn of his profession the funeral director may have been treated with the same disregard, however over time he was able to bill himself as a trained professional capable of performing necessary work in a highly medicalized fashion. Removing the responsibility of this work from the relatives of the deceased would have come as a very welcome service, one that people would be willing to pay well for in order to give their deceased the proper funeral and burial. While death has always been a taboo subject in American society it is also one that has generated a great deal of fascination. Perhaps the greatest unintended consequence of the removal of death from society is that by eliminating the opportunity for firsthand experiences with death (other than our own), we are left to learn how to relate to death from other places. These outlets such as literature, the internet, movies and television have devoted an entire genre of work to the act of death and dying. Typically these works portray death as dark, frightening or tragic (Laderman 2003) or as eroticized (Moller 1996). Since the 1970's horror and "snuff" films have portray torture and death in agonizing detail for the purpose of entertainment. Television shows like HBO's *Six Feet Under* have offered a fictionalized glimpse into the backstage region of the funeral home business; exposing a dark place with troubled people. While this has been the typical manner in which death is presented in our popular culture, it leads us to ask ourselves is death is absent in our culture because of these frightening portrayals or if it is the other way around? Regardless of how it began, each perpetuates the other and furthers the divide between death and American society.

CHAPTER VI
CONCLUSION

The following chapter summarizes the methodology and significant findings. Implications are presented, and future areas of research are suggested. The application of this information to the general public and the implications that the movement may have on the funeral industry is discussed. Finally, I will address the direction that this movement may be heading in the future.

Summary

Data from the AARP 2007 Funeral and Burial Planners Survey was analyzed to better understand support for the green burial movement. Gender, geographic region, age, income and education were used as independent variables. I ran frequencies on each of the six items representing the independent variables and the one representing the dependent variable to insure that the data was clean and to test for reliability then ran cross tabs on each of the independent variables against the dependent variable. Bivariate analyses were used to identify characteristics of supporters of green burial. I found that supporters of green burial were more likely to be female, young (50-59) and living in the South. Supporters were not found to be highly educated, typically having a high school
diploma or some college and earning less than $50,000 per year. Perhaps the most

interesting findings were that support for green burial decreased as education increased and that support was found to be greatest in the South. All of the findings were consistent with previous studies found in the literature with the exception of research on region.

Implications

Application to the General Public

At present this movement represents a little used alternative to traditional burial practices in the U.S. however as land space decreases and environmental concern increases people will be forced to rethink how we use our land and the resources within it. As such traditional burial may cease to be practical or possible and green burial may increase in practice. One important aspect of this movement is that it demystifies death. By promoting burial of a body in a natural state the removal of the elaborate process of embalming and cosmetic alteration is possible. This strips away the "magical illusion" of the funeral (Bartlett and Riches 2007) and leaves individuals face to face with death. This becomes especially so in situations where family elects to participate in the washing and burial of their own loved ones. Adherents of this movement, such as Jerrigrace Lyons, would argue that this close contact with the deceased allows for the reality of death to be more fully grasped by survivors and promotes healthy mourning. Creating spaces where individuals are allowed to have positive interactions with death could have tremendous cultural impact on how society views death and remove some of the fears that we have towards death and dying.

Implications for the Funeral Industry

The data shows that there is significant interest in alternative means of burial, especially among younger, female respondents living in the west. As interest in this movement increases so will the number of facilities offering services to meet the need. Contrary to the controversy over the Mitford book I do not believe that it is the intention of this movement to be considered as an attack on the American funeral industry. While the principles behind green burial are inherently different than traditional burial, it may in fact represent a shift in ideals that the funeral industry will have to eventually embrace. The current burial practices of American society have been in practice for nearly a century however the damage done by these practices will not be sustainable for another. Different methods of burial will be both necessary and inevitable. In general the movement is aiming to improve means of burial not replace the funeral industry. The Green Burial Council works with funeral homes to incorporate green certified practices, such as burial packages that exclude embalming, information on green burial preserves and plain pine or card board boxes for burial, into their current services as another option like cremation.

The Future of the Green Burial Movement

It is a certainty that this movement represents a social phenomenon that will remain as part of the American funeral culture. The individuals discussed in the historic ethnography, in addition to many others, have worked to establish a viable movement in the U.S. and thus far it appears that their efforts have been successful; during the course of this research 5 new natural burial preserves were in the process of being developed and one was opened. The first public green cemetery was opened in Lawrence, KS. With each new cemetery media attention is directed towards the movement thus increasing public awareness of this burial option. This also occurs in conjunction with documentaries and television shows dedicated to the "green movement" in general, as considering this type of burial is considered to be among the "greenest of the green" acts. For those who wish to adhere to the principle of utilizing this method of burial as a means to sustain the planet the future of this movement in the U.S. is likely to lie in promession once it is approved for use. This process has many advantages that make it a desirable option; it is good for the environment, relatively inexpensive and can be utilized to make other burial alternatives such as reef balls or jewelry produced from the carbon found in cremains better for the environment by eliminating the use cremation. While the heart of this movement will always be environmentalism, in the future it will be considered a movement of burial reform. Land is a finite resource; what we have buried into it and how we have used it in the past will continue to effect future generations. Traditional burial as we know it in this country is simply not a sustainable practice. Adherents of the movement have suggested that in the near future traditional burial will viewed as something of a luxury, reserved for a very select few; those who could afford. Much in the same way as the elaborate mummification and burial practices of the ancient Egyptians were considered. As such green burial could become less of an alternative and more of the new burial standard for the average American.

Future Research

This thesis represents an initial investigation into this newly emerging social movement. At the time that this research was conducted there was only one survey instrument available with data specific on this topic. In order to better understand support of this movement a new research tool is needed. Information on support among younger Americans is especially crucial as the AARP survey did not collect data from respondents younger than 50. To fully understand the effect on socioeconomic status on support information on employment would need to be collected and analyzed. A comprehensive tool would also include an independent variable to measures respondent's general attitudes toward mortality in order to ascertain if this influences support for or decision to elect green burial.

Green burial challenges the age old paradigm of conspicuous waste and status display that occur in funerals and burial. The old discourse suggested that lavish and expensive burials were meant to be displays of the wealth and power of the deceased. To do anything less that the most opulent that one could afford would cause the individual in question to loose face. This newly emerging paradigm a perceived connection between what is good for the individual and what is good for the environment. The individual who elects a green burial does not loose face. Future research should explore this emerging ethic and its impact on American burial practices.

REFERENCES

Bartlett, Ruth and Riches, Gordon. 2007. "Magic, Secrets and Grim Reality: Death Work and Boundary Management in the Role of the Funeral Director." *Illness, Crisis and Loss.* 15(3): 233-243.

Bennett, Keith and McBeth, Mark K. 1998. "Contemporary Western Rural USA Economic Composition: Potential Implications for Environmental Policy and Research." *Environmental Management.* 22: 371-381.

Brown, Peggy Ann. "Changing the Paradigm: Historical Trends and the Search for Environmental and Economic Interdependence." *American Forrests.* Spring: 30-35.

Bullard, Robert. 2007. "Dismantling Toxic Racsim." *The Crisis.* July/August: 22-25.

Collins, Wanda and Doolittle, Amy. 2006. "Personal Reflections of Funeral Rites and
Spirituality in a Kentucky African American Family." *Death Studies.* 30(10): 957-969.

Cotgrove, S., and Duff, A. 1980. "Environmentalism, Middle-class Radicalism and Politics." *The Sociological Review.* 2:333-351.

Dalton, R.J., Kuechler, M., and Burklin, W. *Challenging the Political Order: New Social
and Political Movements in Western Democricies.* New York. Oxford University Press.

Davies, Douglas J. 2005. *A Brief History of Death.* Maiden, MA. Blackwell Publishing.

Dunlap, R.E. 1995. *Environmental Politics and Policies.* Durham. Duke University Press.

Eckersley, R. 1989. "Green Politics and the New Class: Selfishness or Virtue?" *Political Studies.* 2: 205-223.

Eternal Reefs a Cremation Memorial Option. Accessed November 15,2008, from

http://vAvw.eternalreefs.com/
Feagan, Robert. 2007. "Death to Life: Toward My Green Burial." *Ethics, Place and Environment.* 10(2): 157-175.

Green Burial Council. Accessed November 15,2008 from http://www.greenburialcouncil.org/

Harvey, Jeff. 2001. "Debunking Myths About Postmortem Care." *Nursing.* 31(7): 44-45.

Hagerman, Chris. 2007. "Shaping Neighborhoods and Nature: Urban Political Ecologies of Urban Waterfront Transformations in Portland, Oregon. *Cities.* 24(4): 285-297.

Hines, Revathi. 2007. "Race, Environmental Justice, and Interest Group Mobilizations: Hazardous Waste and the Case of Sumter County, Alabama." *The Western Journal of Black Studies.* 31(1): 50-57.

Holness, D. Linn abd Nethercott, James R. 1989. "Health Status of Funeral Service Workers Exposed to Formaldehyde." *Archives of Environmental Health.* 44(4): 222-228.

Ho warm, Glennys and Jupp, Peter. (1996) *Contemporary Issues in the Sociology of Death, Dying and Disposal.* New York, NY. St. Martin's Press.

Jones, Robert E., Fly, Mark J., and Cordell, Ken H. 1999 "How Green is my Valley? Tracking Rural and Urban Environmentalism in the Southern Appalachian Ecoregion." *Rural Sociology.* 63(3): 482-499.

Kaufman, Martin. 1998. "Dust to Dust?" *The Environmental Magazine.* 9(6): 17-21.

Kriesi, H. 1989. "New Social Movements and the New Class in the Netherlands." *American Journal of Sociology.* 94: 1078-1116.

Laderman, Gary. 2000. "The Disney Way of Death." *The American Academy of Religion.* 68(1): 27-46.

Laderman, Gary. 2003. *Rest in Peace: A Cultural History of Death and the Funeral Home in Twentieth-Century America.* Oxford New York. Oxford University Press.

McCausland, Janet. 2008. "Burial Out of a Box." *Alternative Journals.* 34:1-6

McNally, Patrick. 2007. Promession: Return to Living Soil. *The Daily Undertaker A Funeral.* Accessed March 25, 2009, from hppt://thedailyundertaker.com/ and Memorial Service Journal. Retrieved April 5,2009, from http://www.dailyundertaker.com/2008/09/promession-return-to-living-soil.html

Mertig, Angela, and Dunlap, Riley. 2001. "Environmentalism, New Social Movements, and the New Class: A Cross-National Investigation." *Rural Sociology.* 66(1):113-136.

Memorial Ecosystems. Retrieved March 7, 2009, from http://www.memorialecosystems.com/

Moller, David Wendell. 1996. *Confronting Death: Values, Institutions and Human Mortality.* New York, NY. Oxford University Press.

Morrison, D.E., and Dunlap, R.E. 1986. "Environmentalism and Elitism: a Conceptual and Empirical Analysis. *Environmental Management.* 10:581-589.

Nas, Masja, and Dekker, Paul. 1996. "Environmental Involvement in Four West European Countries: A Comparative Analysis of Attitudes and Actions. *Innovation: The European Journal of Social Sciences.* 9(4): 509-535.

Promessa Organic. Retrieved April 5, 2009, from http://promessa.se/index_en.asp

Reis, Joao Jose. 2003. *Death is a Festival: Funeral Rites and Rebellion in Nineteenth-Century Brazil.* Chapel Hill and London. The University of North Carolina Press.

Sappol, Michael. 2002. *Traffic of Dead Bodies.* Princeton and Oxford. Princeton University Press.

Skogen, Ketil. 1996. "Young Environmentalists: Post-modern Identities or Middle-class Culture?" *The Editorial Board of the Sociological Review.* 452-473.

Stowe, J.R., Johnny; Schmidt, Elsie V., and Green, Deborah. 2001. "Toxic Burials: The Final Insult." *Conservative Biology.* 15(6): 1817-1819.

Stubbe, Bill. 2007. *Death Midwifery and the Home Funeral Revolution.* Accessed January 21, 2009, from http://forrest of memories.org.media/2007/03/30/deathmidwifery-and-the-home-funeral-industy.com/

Tindall, D.B., Davies, Scott, and Mauboules, Celine. 2003. "Activism and Conservation Behaviors in an Environmental Movement: The contradictory Effects of Gender." *Society and Nature.* 16: 909-932.

Voekel, Pamela. 2002. *Alone Before God: The Religious Origins of Modernity in Mexico.* Durham and London. Duke University Press.

Will de Chaparro, Martina. 2007. *Death and Dying in New Mexico.* Albuquerque, NM. University of New Mexico Press.

Wirzba, Norman. 2003. *The Essential Agrarian Reader.* Lexington, KY. The University

Press of Kentucky.

i want morebooks!

Buy your books fast and straightforward online - at one of world's fastest growing online book stores! Environmentally sound due to Print-on-Demand technologies.

Buy your books online at
www.get-morebooks.com

Kaufen Sie Ihre Bücher schnell und unkompliziert online – auf einer der am schnellsten wachsenden Buchhandelsplattformen weltweit! Dank Print-On-Demand umwelt- und ressourcenschonend produziert.

Bücher schneller online kaufen
www.morebooks.de

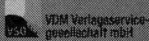 VDM Verlagsservicegesellschaft mbH
Heinrich-Böcking-Str. 6-8   Telefon: +49 681 3720 174   info@vdm-vsg.de
D - 66121 Saarbrücken   Telefax: +49 681 3720 1749   www.vdm-vsg.de

Made in the USA
Columbia, SC
28 October 2020

MAN MEETS METAL

Richard Platt

Illustrated by Yannick Robert

OXFORD
UNIVERSITY PRESS

Contents

PART 1
The Stone Age — 6

PART 2
The Bronze Age — 12

PART 3
The Iron Age — 26

Glossary — 30

Index — 31

10 000 BCE   9000 BCE   8000 BCE   7000 BCE   6000 BCE   50

Ancient Britain
10 000 BCE – 4200 BCE

Ancient Britain

In the distant past, Britain changed from an empty island to a green home for a busy farming people. This is the story of how Britain began.

Britain's first people walked here 12 000 years ago, when Britain was still connected to Europe.

My grandfather says the animals we chase are smaller than the deer and horses he used to catch. This makes them harder to hunt. To kill them, we have to shape stone into better weapons. We also get food from the sea now. We catch fish with spears and gather creatures with shells.

4000 BCE — 3000 BCE — 2000 BCE — 1000 BCE — 0

Stone Age
4200 BCE – 2500 BCE

Bronze Age
2500 BCE – 800 BCE

Iron Age
800 BCE – 60 BCE

By 5500 BCE, the ice sheets that once covered northern Britain had melted. The sea rose. Britain became an island, and forests grew.

Experts guess that just 20 000 people **roamed** around Britain, living in movable camps.

In the Stone Age, people made tools and weapons from stone. Later, in the Bronze Age and Iron Age, they began to use metals.

5

10 000 BCE   9000 BCE   8000 BCE   7000 BCE   6000 BCE   50

Ancient Britain
10 000 BCE – 4200 BCE

PART 1

The Stone Age

Hunters to Farmers

Britain's first people got plenty to eat by travelling round to hunt and gather food. But then, about 6000 years ago, they stopped roaming. They had found a different way to get food: farming.

Within just 300 years, most Britons had settled near the fields where they farmed.

Ancient Britain
10 000 BCE – 4200 BCE

Craftsmen and Potters

Britons learned about new materials and skills from strangers who came from Europe in boats.

I made this axe out of a hard green rock called jadeite. Jadeite comes from the Alps, a range of mountains about 1000 kilometres away, and shaping and polishing this rock takes many weeks. This means my jadeite axe is too good to use for chopping things. It will be used as money, or to show off.

It was hard to get rocks that were good for tool-making. Stone-workers found them in Cornwall, Cumbria and Norfolk, but they were rare.

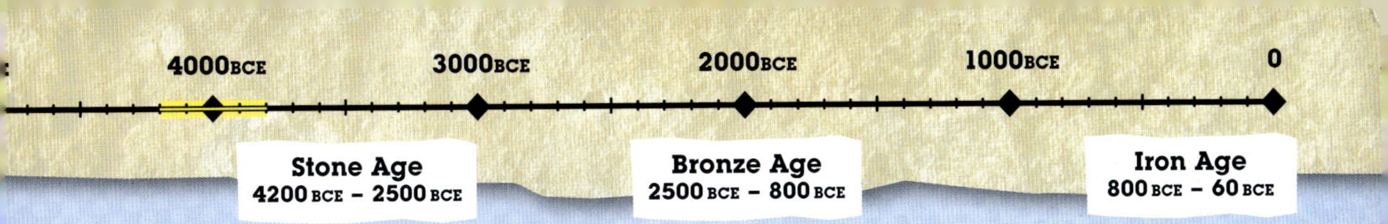

| 4000 BCE | 3000 BCE | 2000 BCE | 1000 BCE | 0 |

Stone Age
4200 BCE – 2500 BCE

Bronze Age
2500 BCE – 800 BCE

Iron Age
800 BCE – 60 BCE

Britons also learned how to shape clay into pots. They decorated them by pressing patterns into the clay. Then they heated the pots in a fire to harden them.

Ancient Britain
10 000 BCE – 4200 BCE

Builders

Neolithic people built amazing earth and stone structures. They arranged mounds and upright rocks to form circles and straight lines. These were places to perform **rituals** or to talk to their gods.

| 4000 BCE | 3000 BCE | 2000 BCE | 1000 BCE | 0 |

Stone Age
4200 BCE – 2500 BCE

Bronze Age
2500 BCE – 800 BCE

Iron Age
800 BCE – 60 BCE

These ancient people also built stone tombs for the dead.

Archaeologists have learned a lot from the **preserved** bones. Stone-Age people were a little shorter than modern-day people.

Now that our lives are safer and more settled, we can build better, stronger houses. Look at this great hall! It has room inside for 25 people. Our leaders live well in halls like this, and all our families can gather in them.

10 000 BCE   9000 BCE   8000 BCE   7000 BCE   6000 BCE   50

Ancient Britain 10 000 BCE – 4200 BCE

PART 2

THE BRONZE AGE

Beakers and Blades

About 4500 years ago, Britons saw metal for the first time – and they were impressed. Copper axes made it easier to cut down trees and clear land.

> Men from across the sea landed here not long ago with new and exciting things. They had amazing axes that were not made of stone! I have seen one myself: its smooth blade shines in the sun. It does not break easily, as a stone axe does. Just rubbing it on a rock makes the blade sharp!

| 4000 BCE | 3000 BCE | 2000 BCE | 1000 BCE | 0 |

Stone Age
4200 BCE – 2500 BCE

Bronze Age
2500 BCE – 800 BCE

Iron Age
800 BCE – 60 BCE

As well as metal axes, the strangers also brought beautiful pottery. Archaeologists have called them the 'Beaker people' after the fine drinking cups they made.

10 000 BCE   9000 BCE   8000 BCE   7000 BCE   6000 BCE

Ancient Britain
10 000 BCE – 4200 BCE

Miraculous Metal

Today, many metal things are common and cheap, but 3000 years ago they were rare and precious. Compared to wood, bone and stone, metal seemed like amazing stuff.

Although foreigners brought the first metal things, Britons soon found places to dig up their own metal. There were copper mines in Ireland by 2400 BCE, and in Wales soon after. In Cornwall they dug for tin. With these two metals, they could make bronze.

Bronze tools were difficult to make. Many centuries passed before they replaced stone tools.

Ancient Britain
10 000 BCE – 4200 BCE

Awesome Bronze Age Stuff

Owning shiny, rare stuff has always been a sure way to show off. In the Bronze Age it wasn't the latest phone that everyone wanted. It was jewellery made from rare stones and anything metal.

These precious things were signs of power. They were very unusual, or came from very far away. Only important people could own them.

Ancient Britain
10 000 BCE – 4200 BCE

Sailing Heroes

Around Britain's coasts, there was a new kind of hero: the sailor. Sailors were fearless adventurers.

Look at my boat. Isn't it fine? I cut planks of wood and sewed them together with tough **tree fibres**. A boat like this can sail further than those old ones made from skin and sticks. You still have to paddle it carefully, though. Big waves can sink it, so I only go to sea in good weather.

| 4000 BCE | 3000 BCE | 2000 BCE | 1000 BCE | 0 |

Stone Age
4200 BCE – 2500 BCE

Bronze Age
2500 BCE – 800 BCE

Iron Age
800 BCE – 60 BCE

With sharp bronze tools they built new kinds of boats. By 2000 BCE, sailors were competing with each other. Who could travel the furthest – and come back alive?

During the next five centuries, boats became more and more common.

The **climate** was warmer and crops grew better. Everyone tried to get the best land so they could grow extra food. When their **rivalry** turned to war, villages became forts. Fences and ditches kept out enemies.

Ancient Britain
10 000 BCE – 4200 BCE

Honouring the Gods

Bronze Age Britons believed that gods ruled their lives, luck and land. Sometimes they offered bronze axes as costly gifts for the gods.

As the changing climate ruined crops, many people threw their axes into the water. They hoped this would bring better harvests.

10 000 BCE   9000 BCE   8000 BCE   7000 BCE   6000 BCE   50

Ancient Britain
10 000 BCE – 4200 BCE

PART 3

The Iron Age

Tools and Weapons from Europe

Originally a land of forests and wild places, Britain was now covered in fields and tracks. Crops grew and animals grazed on almost every piece of flat, low land. Stones cleared from the fields were heaped in lines to make walls.

Farming families lived in large round houses. Nearby were barns, animal pens and grain stores.

The people who lived and worked there had strong links to nearby countries. Their clothes, pots and tools looked like those used all over nearby Europe, and lots of people had come from Europe to live in Britain.

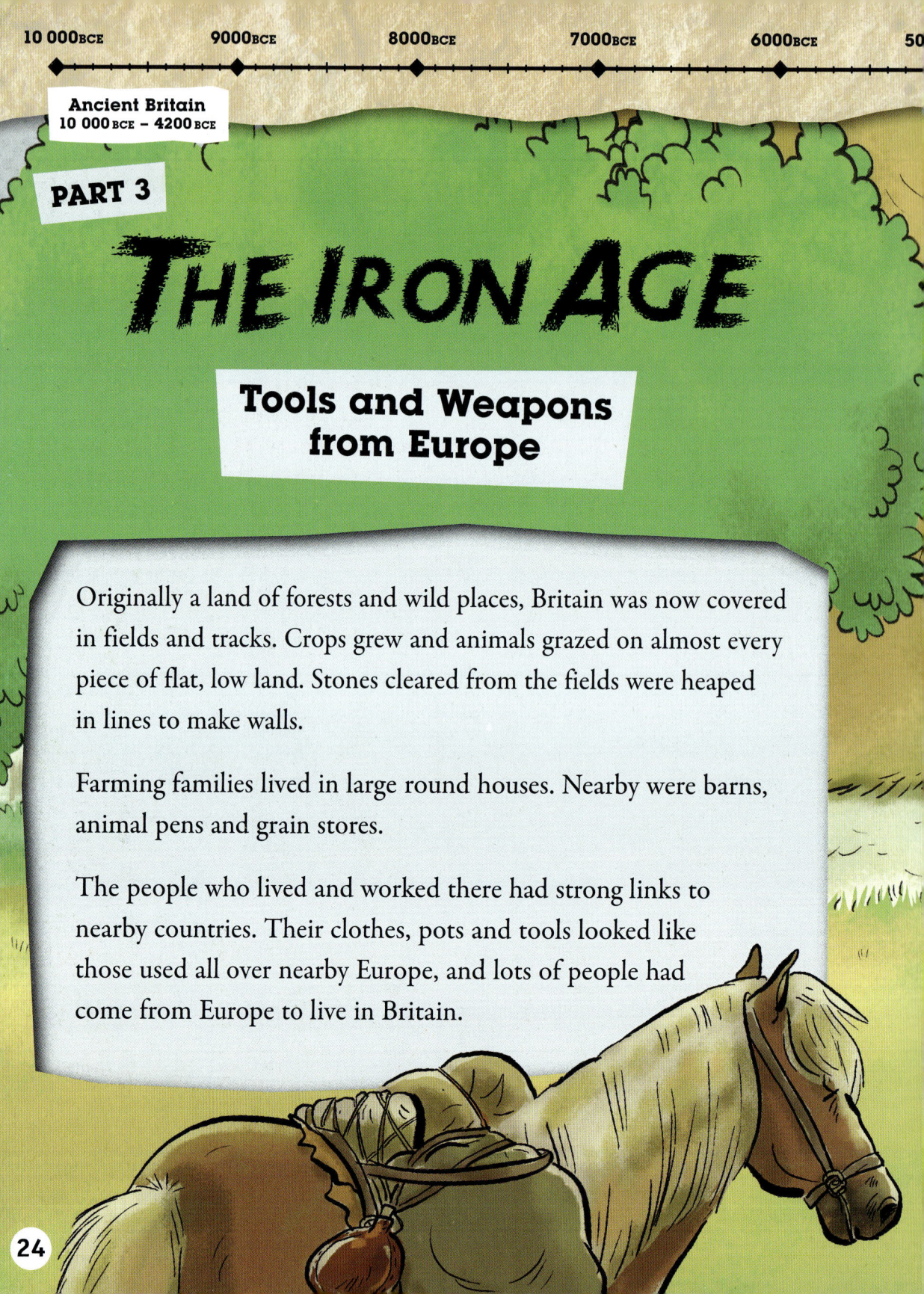

Ancient Britain
10 000 BCE – 4200 BCE

Sharper, Lighter, Deadlier

The new tools and weapons gave this time period its name: the Iron Age. Iron was a more useful metal than bronze, but it was harder to make.

Only a few clever blacksmiths knew the secret. Their skills earned them fame. They beat glowing lumps of iron into swords with special patterns. Their weapons were one of the first fashions of the Iron Age.

| 10 000 BCE | 9000 BCE | 8000 BCE | 7000 BCE | 6000 BCE |

Ancient Britain
10 000 BCE – 4200 BCE

Chariots and Hill Forts

On a windy hilltop, a busy village is protected by grassy banks. Suddenly the gates open and a line of chariots speeds out.

CHARGE! We are the bravest of our people – and the wealthiest, too! With our horses, armour and chariots, we fight off rivals and keep the hill fort safe. We risk our lives to earn riches and honour.

| 4000 BCE | 3000 BCE | 2000 BCE | 1000 BCE | 0 |

Stone Age
4200 BCE – 2500 BCE

Bronze Age
2500 BCE – 800 BCE

Iron Age
800 BCE – 60 BCE

Despite their power, Britain's warriors eventually faced a stronger **foe**. From 55 BCE, Roman armies from Italy began to arrive in Britain. Within 100 years, the Romans had conquered much of the country. They lived here for three centuries and wrote about the country and people they ruled.

For Britain, it was the beginning of a brand new period of history.

29

Glossary

archaeologists: people who dig up the remains of the past

amber: hardened tree juice that looks like clear yellow plastic

chariots: carriages with two wheels pulled by horses, used in ancient races and battles

climate: the type of weather that a particular area has

foe: an enemy or opponent

furnace: a space for heating up metal or glass

plough blades: large pieces of metal which are used to prepare fields for growing crops

jet: a black rock used to make jewellery

preserved: something which has lasted and not rotted away

rituals: special actions which early Britons performed to please their gods

rivalry: competition to be the best

roamed: moved, travelled or wandered over a wide area

tree fibres: pieces of tree roots or branches that can be used as ropes

Index

axes 7, 8, 12–13, 15, 22–23

boats 8, 18–19

chariots 28

copper 12, 14–15

farming 6–7, 24

feasts 20

gods 10, 22

houses 11, 24

hunting 4, 6

iron 25–27

jewellery 16–17

pottery 9, 13, 24

Romans 29

stone circles 10

tombs 11

warriors 17, 20, 28–29

About the author

I have written more than 100 books, most of them information books for children. I became interested in Ancient Britain after going on a Stone-Age skills course, where I lit a fire and made stone arrowheads and rope. I think I could have just about survived 10 000 years ago, though I don't think I would have liked the food!

Not all of my work is for children. I've also written TV scripts, restaurant reviews, and jokes for museum videos. When I am not writing, I enjoy rock climbing, cycling and mending clocks.

Greg Foot, Series Editor

I've loved science ever since the day I took my papier mâché volcano into school. I filled it with far too much baking powder, vinegar and red food colouring, and WHOOSH! I covered the classroom ceiling in red goo. Now I've got the best job in the world: I present TV shows for the BBC, answer kids' science questions on YouTube, and make huge explosions on stage at festivals!

Working on TreeTops inFact has been great fun. There are so many brilliant books, and guess what ... they're all packed full of awesome facts! What's your favourite?